D0819679

Croft, Hurworth, Neasham, Middleton and Dinsdale
in old picture postcards

by Vera Chapman

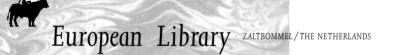

European Library ZALTBOMMEL / THE NETHERLANDS

GB ISBN 90 2886347 8
© 1996 European Library – Zaltbommel/The Netherlands
Second edition, 1997: reprint of the original edition of 1996.

No part of this book may be reproduced in any form, by print, photoprint,
microfilm or any other means, without written permission from the publisher.

Introduction

The neighbouring villages of Croft, Hurworth, Neasham, Middleton and Dinsdale lie along the river Tees about three miles south of Darlington in County Durham. In places they merge into one another. Croft, Hurworth and Neasham are virtually a continuum, whilst Middleton St. George and Middleton One Row in fact are. Only Dinsdale is separate and rural. But what happened in the parish of Dinsdale affected Middleton One Row on the other side of the boundary, and oddly, the railway station serving the two Middletons is named Dinsdale!

These five villages share a variety of common experiences. Their river and countryside provide recreation for residents, for townspeople and for visitors, fishermen, ramblers, naturalists and golfers. The Tees, that 'boiling, surging water' of Celtic name, at times thundered down in spate from the Pennines as a wall of water, the Tees Roll. It wrought havoc over the centuries upon Teesbank settlements in repeated inundations.

The villages commonly look to Darlington as their market town, shopping centre and workplace. In return, the villages developed as residential and retirement places, not only for Darlington but also, from the mid-nineteenth century, for the growing industrial centres of Teesside. At first it was for wealthier families with their villas, but latterly on a wider basis. A further link between the villages came with the dawn of steam-hauled public railway transport for goods and passengers. The Stockton and Darlington Railway opened via Fighting Cocks in 1825 and its Croft Branch came to Hurworth Place in 1829.

Historically a part of County Durham and the land of the Prince Bishops, four of the five villages came administratively into Darlington Rural District. From the reorganisation of local government in 1974, the Rural District was united with the County Borough of Darlington to become one of the eight Districts of County Durham. From 1997, Darlington and its surrounding villages are to become an independent Unitary Authority.

Croft might appear to be the odd one out, being historically in the North Riding of Yorkshire, and from 1974 in Richmondshire, a District of North Yorkshire. But Croft-on-Tees has been linked from medieval times by the sturdy but graceful bridge which carries the Great North Road onward to Darlington and sends a road directly to Hurworth-on-Tees, Neasham and Middleton. Croft also shared the railway experience, being connected to Darlington from the Durham end of Croft Bridge by the Croft Branch of the S&DR from 1829, and by the Great North of England Railway from York to Darlington from 1841.

Moreover, the birth of Croft as a spa in the 17th century and its expansion following the New Spa of 1829, meant that both Croft and Hurworth Place redeveloped at either end of the bridge to serve the Spa. Hurworth Place additionally grew to serve the railway, coal sidings and gas works. In fact, the main line station on the Hurworth side was at first named Croft and later Croft Spa! Dinsdale, too, developed a Spa similar in sulphurous content to that at Croft, but it succumbed at an earlier date. Both villages are now small and rural, and have maintained a strong, probably a predominant, farming interest.

Formerly there were other populous settlements. Croft had two manors. The medieval villages of Middleton St. George, West Hartburn and Dinsdale, however, disappeared when their common arable fields were enclosed in the 16th and 17th centuries. Only grassy bumps and hollows remain. Over Middleton, later renamed Middleton-One-Row, and Croft shrank, but filled out again later when their spas were established.

The central villages expanded to become the largest in this group of five, redeveloping with manufacturing. Hurworth-on-Tees and Neasham prospered for a while with the cottage hand-loom weaving of linen for Darlington merchants. Middleton St. George redeveloped with ironworks and ancillary industries. These were concentrated at a new location beside the Stockton and Darlington Railway some distance away from the medieval site beside the old parish church. Then the Second World War brought a shift eastward at Goosepool airfield, now Teesside International Airport, and new uses for the old airfield buildings. Middleton-One-Row revived to serve Dinsdale spa with lodgings and went on to expand with desirable residences.

So these five villages tributary to Darlington share similarities and diversities of past experience. They also share with previous generations, glimpsed in these pictures between the 1880s and the 1930s, the beautiful countryside and attractive river banks along the spectacular curves of the winding Tees.

1 Croft Bridge has withstood ferocious Tees floods for centuries. A bridge here was repaired in 1356. The red sandstone structure visible today on the downstream side dates from the 15th century. An inscribed Blue Stone of Frosterley marble records its restoration in 1673. The catastrophic flood of 1771 meant more repairs, followed in 1795 by widening upstream in the hard brown sandstone seen here. Croft Bridge carried the Great North Road, turnpiked in 1745, from Yorkshire into County Durham where the first bridge-end toll-house was swept away in the 1753 flood. Tolls ended in 1879 and the toll house became, for a while, a smithy. At Croft Bridge or Neasham ford until 1826, each new Prince Bishop of Durham was handed the falchion, the sword with which Sir John Conyers slew a dragon, the Sockburn Worm. Bishop David Jenkins revived the ceremony. The flood wall and seats have gone.

Croft Spa Bridge.

2　This winter crowd scene on a postcard posted in 1909 is at the Yorkshire end of Croft Bridge. St. Peter's Church chancel appears on the left. Bunting winds up the two telegraph poles and is slung across the bridge approach. The picture could have been taken at an unveiling of the granite plaque to commemorate Queen Victoria's Diamond Jubilee, 1897, on the upstream parapet at the Croft end of the bridge. Or was it for a falchion ceremony for an incoming new Bishop of Durham, or were they waiting to greet a royal visitor?

3   This turn-of-the-century view of the parish church of St. Peter, Croft-on-Tees, was taken from below the bridge-end. The two pale gravestones, now darkened, were then new, the smaller being dated 1899. The photograph also captured the rebuilt upper tower, its new battlements and the new east window of the south aisle, all part of a Victorian restoration of 1878. The prominent Gothic gravestone no longer stands and the rails have gone from the table tombs below the chancel's east window. The background trees are now much larger, and those along the river obscure this view of the church formerly visible whilst crossing Croft Bridge. Like the older side of the bridge, the church was built from the red sandstone which outcrops along the river Tees between Croft and Dinsdale.

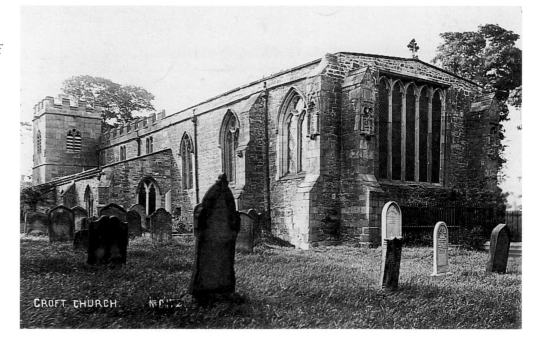

CROFT CHURCH.   N°[?] 2

4   A postcard made from this original picture was posted in 1910. The elevated Milbank pew, overhanging both nave and north aisle, has for long vied to dominate the interior of Croft church. The Milbanks acquired the Place family's Halnaby estate in Croft and took the 14th century north aisle for their burials. In the background, the white marble chest tomb surmounted by a funeral helm is that of Sir Mark Milbank who died in 1680. The audacious 17th century family pew was probably used by Lord Byron and his bride Annabella (Anne Isabella) Milbank when they honeymooned in 1815 at Halnaby Hall. In 1857 the Wilson Todds bought the Halnaby estate, and at the end of the Second World War gave the pew to the church. Halnaby Hall was demolished in 1952.

MILBANK PEW, CROFT CHURCH.

5   Croft village consists of several terraces, scattered cottages, two halls, a hotel and the old rectory. Still embowered in trees, a modicum of later housing is insufficient to change the village's character. Monkend Lane leads past Monkend Terrace and Monkend Hall to Croft Mill. On the left, opposite the church where the Reverend Charles Dodgson served 1843-1868, are the rectory gardens. Here ran a model railway, topical because of the recent arrival of the Croft Branch and North of England railways. The Rector's eldest son, Charles Ludwidge Dodgson (Lewis Carroll), entertained the many children of the family, creating stories, magazines and games. The grinning cat on Croft church sedilia and the Sockburn Worm are amongst local inspirations which emerged in his 'Alice' books.

6   The eight houses of Monkend Terrace were built in pairs of slightly varying styles. The pair beyond the window cleaner are reached by railed steps, as on the previous picture, and have a date plaque 1865. Monkend Terrace, South Parade, Richmond Terrace, The Terrace and South Terrace are thought to have been built as lodging houses to serve Croft Spa. Up to the 1930s and until the Second World War, lodgings were offered at Croft and at Hurworth Place across the river. Monkend Lane led to the water corn mill on Clow Beck, near which some new houses have just been unobtrusively sited.

7   This railed avenue of ancient trees fronting Monkend Hall was felled a few years ago and replanted with fast-growing Lombardy poplars, now impressively tall. Behind the poplars is a new avenue of chestnuts which will mature in the longer term. Land at Monkend belonged to St. Mary's monastery, York, and was bought after the Dissolution by Roland Place of Halnaby. Possibly it was he who built the old stone house which survives behind the brick façade of circa 1730. Here, after his retirement sale in 1810 lived Charles Colling, famous Shorthorn breeder from Ketton Hall, whose bull Comet fetched 1,000 guineas. Monkend Hall was for half a century the home of Captain Parlour who died in 1977. The windows have now been restored with more appropriate small panes.

8　Croft Mill, a water-powered corn mill, was granted after the Conquest to Sir Hammon Clervaux whose family held it for sixteen generations. The little Clow Beck turned Jolby Mill and Croft Mill before entering the Tees upstream of Croft Bridge. The present mill was built on the embankment which ponded back a mill dam or reservoir. It was last worked by William Adamson until 1947, when the dam burst and drained direct to the Tees instead of through the mill. Repairs seemed too costly for what then appeared to be a dying trade. Mr. Adamson continued to farm there, however, with swallows nesting in the rafters and a dipper by the wheel. Limewash hid the red sandstone rubble walling which by the 1960s was showing through and has now been made a feature in the conversion of the mill into a house.

9   South Parade was confusingly also called Monk's End. It was formerly known as Kidling Croft Lane and led over a packhorse bridge to Stapleton. Rectory Lane emerges on the right. Here the wall encloses an orchard for the end house of South Terrace against whose gable a fruit tree is trained. Four newer houses now continue South Terrace over this site. On the left is the gable end and bellcote of the old village school designed by the Durham architect Ignatius Bonomi. It was built in 1845 on glebe land given by the rector, the Ven. Charles Dodgson, and is now offices. The playground fence, large tree and hedge-bank have gone. A new post-war school has been built behind the school-teacher's house of 1850 on the left, part of whose garden was taken to extend the old school playground.

10   Croft Spa Hotel, built in 1835 by Sir William Chaytor and designed by Ignatius Bonomi, replaced the Black Bull. The hotel catered for New Spa visitors with a billiard room, reading room, smoking room and ballroom or assembly room. Travellers 'stopped for a meal and to take the Spa waters which were said to make men vigorous and women fruitful'. In the hotel's early days boarding was 1½ guineas a week and an extra ½ guinea for a private sitting room. Towards the end of the century under the Winteringhams the hotel prospered. There was fishing, a stud of thoroughbreds, hunters were stabled, waggonettes, broughams and phaetons were for hire. Four packs of hounds met at Croft and the stable yard became a horses' cemetery. The wooden churchyard gates have now given way to ornate iron gates and an overthrow arch. The big tree hiding the tower has been felled, but yews now obscure the porch.

11 A quiet scene along the Northallerton road. Horse droppings on roads were a problem, especially on dry windy days. The grassy patches on the left used to be a continuous area known as Smugglers Green. Suspicion centered on a local barn. The brick house behind the wall, re-named The Poplars, was Bridge House, until recently the home of Miss Chaytor, who told the author it was built about 1770 by a stone mason! Richmond Lane leads off to the right just beyond the telegraph poles and passes Croft Hall, the ancient seat of the Clervaux and Chaytor families, which was refronted in the 18th century. It became for a while a boarding school for about thirty young ladies aged 8-18 after the Chaytors moved to Clervaux Castle.

12   Clervaux Castle with its six square towers dominated a park of 160 acres between the Jolby and Richmond Roads. It was designed in a neo-Norman style by Ignatius Bonomi and built in 1840-1843 by Sir William Chaytor, recently created a baronet. He died in 1847. His widow Isabella and two daughters continued to live there attended by five house servants. With twelve bedrooms and four reception rooms, the castle was noted for its fine plasterwork and oak panelling, screen and magnificent staircase brought from the Newcastle Mansion House. In 1918 the contents were offered for sale, the Chaytor family having moved back into Croft Hall. After military occupation during the Second World War, the castle was demolished in 1955, but the gate lodge and woodland remain.

Clervaux Castle   Valentines Series

13   Looking north from the Richmond Lane junction, this faded picture reveals old cottages along the Tees bank. Others to the right, including the former Black Bull coaching inn converted to cottages, were demolished when new post-war villas were built along the riverside. At the turn of the century, Croft was referred to as the Queen of Yorkshire Villages. The roadside seat was one of several on the walks to the Old and New Spa wells. Richmond Lane 'well supplied with rustic seats under the shade of trees' led to the Old Spa. On the way it passed Richmond Terrace, where the last house was once a grocer's shop. Across the lane, the Terrace was built as spa lodgings, but is now four houses, beyond which is South Terrace.

CROFT VILLAGE.   Nº 173

14   This picture is enlarged from an old souvenir photograph frame. Can the gutted building at Old Spa Farm beside the Spa Beck have been this? People had begun to bathe in the Stinking Pits known to cure cattle and horses, so circa 1670 Sir William Chaytor built here a cold Bath House. By the early 18th century bottled water was being sold in London. Yet by the mid-19th century 'nothing could be more primitive or of ruder aspect'. A pipe from the source fed the bath at a constant 51°F and a tank outside, from which visitors 'drank three to seven half-pint tumblers', finding the water strongly diuretic. Sulphur deposits encrusted the surroundings. Later, the Sweet Well was found in the wood to the north and the Canny Well to the south. By this time, however, a new well had been bored in 1827 and the New Spa established.

OLD BATHS, CROFT.

15   A woodland walk along Spa Beck connected the Old and New Spas. The Canny Well spring rose in these woods and was piped to the cold plunge bath at the New Spa. The direct route from the village was via Richmond Lane, up a few stone steps and alongside Croft Hall grounds, through the high side of Echo Field where wooden benches allowed a rest, and into the New Spa drive. A double or even treble echo came from the four-arched skew bridge which, from 1841, carried the railway over the Tees. The workmen boring in 1827 for Sir William Chaytor's new well, fled when the water burst forth with great force. It rivalled Harrogate in sulphur content, and numerous analyses of Croft waters were made. They were believed to alleviate rheumatism, gout and ailments of the digestive system, kidneys, liver and skin complaints.

16　The New Spa designed by Ignatius Bonomi was opened in 1829. This picture is also taken from the wooden souvenir photograph frame. Croquet was in progress in front of the Bath House, with the coach house and keeper's cottage alongside. Behind the verandah was the central pump room. The strongly sulphurous water emerged from the New Well at a constant temperature of 52°F, and was drunk with an added teaspoonful of common salt if warmed. Opening off a long corridor behind were six warm baths lined with Dutch tiles, a vapour bath, a cold plunge bath lined with stone flags and paved with slate, an attendant's room and a boiler room. With each bath was a dressing room. 'All the doors painted white lead colour developed a jet black coating from the effluvia'. Silver became tarnished.

NEW BATHS, CROFT.

17   In Edwardian times the trellised verandah of the New Spa was festooned with roses and rustic seats. A penny in the slot music box played 'Whisper and I shall Hear' and 'Boys of the Old Brigade'! The water came opaque like jellyfish, turned milky white on exposure to air and left a sulphurous deposit. A half-pint was to be drunk two or three times a day. The dressing rooms had carpets, chairs, dressing tables, mirrors and clean white walls. The 'husbands' train' reunited businessmen's families who stayed for weeks on end. The Visitors' Book named the entire Sunderland Football Team of 1901.

In the 1920s daily bus excursions ran from Tyneside. Opening at 7 a.m., hot sulphur baths cost 2/-, cold baths 9d, the cold plunge 6d and water 2d per glass.

By the late 1950s, however, when the proprietress died, it was little used, closed soon afterwards and was demolished.

18   Across the Tees from Croft, Hurworth Place in the parish of Hurworth and county of Durham was often called Croft or Croft Spa, no doubt because many of the houses took in spa visitors, some of whom arrived by train on this side of the river. The low-lying road here suffered regular flooding, which has continued from time to time despite massive embanking and the construction of the Cow Green controlling reservoir in the upper reaches of the Tees since this picture was taken. In the great flood of 1771, the family at the Slip Inn along the Darlington Road escaped within three minutes of being drowned. Their neighbour William Allison at Oxen-le-Fields Farm suffered water six feet high in the house and lost two fat cattle, five horses and a ram. An old couple in Croft clung to their roof ridge until able to drop safely, and the church was inundated.

Tees River in Flood, Croft Spa

19   The roads from Hurworth, Darlington and Northallerton converge on the County Durham end of Croft Bridge, whose upstream parapet just appears on the picture. Seats encircle the trees behind the fence. This leisurely scene contrasts strongly with the swirl of traffic today. The Comet Hotel displays the Cyclists' Touring Club bicycle wheel sign. The inn sign represents the bull 'Comet', which was bought by a consortium of four local farmers when its breeder Charles Colling of Ketton Hall Farm retired in 1810 and came to live at Monkend Hall in Croft. It was the first bull to reach that price. The old Comet signboard went to the Harrisons at Gainford Hall, another family of Shorthorn breeders.

CROFT SPA.   Nº1112

20　The pleasant doorways of the Comet Hotel are in evidence here. The gas lamp on the main porch reflects the fact that the Croft and Hurworth Gas Company in 1856 established their gas works near the rear of the hotel. The works were beside a coal depot and the terminus of the S&DR Croft Branch line which carried coal for delivery into Yorkshire. The Croft Branch of 1829 was superseded in 1841 at a higher level by the Great North of England Railway from York to Darlington, now the main London to Edinburgh line. The gas works supplied public lighting for Hurworth, Hurworth Place and Croft. The sharp bend of the river Tees is reflected in the curve of the Darlington road and of the railings which guard a sudden drop into the river down the flood wall.

21   The Comet Hotel faces the bridge-end, whilst South View continues along the Darlington road, housing the shop and post office. Hurworth Place developed with the arrival of the railways. Terraces housing railway workers and artisans grew up along the Hurworth Road, with the Railway hotel, a Methodist Chapel and the more substantial Banks Terrace facing its own garden square. By the 1890s, eleven houses were offering lodgings. The flood wall with the river lapping at its foot show clearly in this picture, where now a grassed flood bank and gentle slope down to the river occupy much of the foreground.

CROFT, SOUTH VIEW.   Nº 0564

22   South View curves towards the confluence of the Skerne with the Tees. On the left, built of cream brick and set back in gardens, are Croft House and its outbuildings. The latter were converted into Tees View Cottages, an intriguing crescent of castellated dwellings with patterned brickwork. They back on to the former Croft Branch railway of 1829, now only a cinder track. The main line is at a higher level behind, on the horizon. Numerous people are using the seats round the trees. The flood of January 1995 reached the summit of the present graded and grassed protective embankment. It swept round to invade the walled garden in the angle between the Tees and the Skerne. It also invaded the cellars of Monkend Terrace and Croft Mill on the opposite bank. Tees is an old British river name, Tesa or Teisa, meaning boiling surging river!

23   The station at Hurworth Place, seen here in 1889, was known as Croft until renamed Croft Spa in 1896. It closed in 1969 when the Richmond Branch line closed. The main line continued at this level to cross the Tees by the skew bridge of the 1841 Great North of England Railway. Note the numerous gas lamps and the gardens, a competitive feature at NER stations. The southbound train has just passed under a footbridge carrying Hurworth back lane down to the Darlington road. A train journey to London in 1906 took about five hours. The wooden steps in the left corner led to a separate station footbridge next to the Hurworth road bridge behind the photographer. The footbridge disappeared when the height of the road bridge was raised in 1959-60 in expectation of the electrification of the East Coast route. After a thirty year wait, 225 electrics now hurtle through the closed station.

24   The steep slope up from Croft Bridge-end at Hurworth Place to the station is captured here, with Croft Bridge in the background. Today, the downhill slope and curve catch out motorists, and the low garden walls on the left have been damaged. The slope is made obvious by the differences in height between the houses on opposite sides of the road. Most of the older houses in the villages downstream of Darlington are of brick made from the local clay left by glaciers at the end of the Ice Age. The red Triassic sandstone found in the river bed is rather soft, but in early times this and river cobbles were used for building.

CROFT SPA.

25   Rounding the sharp bend in the previous picture, the Hurworth Road levels out at the railway bridge. Between the bridge wall-end on the right and the shop is the entrance ramp and footbridge to the station, now all gone. The shop is Carnaby's Provision Store, and appears to display household hardware. On the left, John Wilson has a grocery, and has been there from the 1890s. The card was posted in 1905. Next door is the Station Hotel, next to which the recess began a footpath which crossed the railway lines and continued through fields past Pilmoor to Blind Lane. Because of danger from today's main line train speeds, the path has been diverted.

Croft Spa Village

3933

26   Mrs. Sarah Newton was a grocer at Hurworth Place in the 1890s. She was an agent for Pullars of Perth dry cleaning and prominently advertised in enamelled lettering on her shop windows: Fry's Pure Cocoa and Fry's Chocolate by Royal appointment with 300 prize medals. Park, the butcher's shop next door, appears to be unoccupied. Station Terrace is probably of mid-19th century date, with bays added later. The next two premises now have newer bay windows. Above the imposing portico a large signboard reads 'Refreshments'. Once on the level, the road leads on to Hurworth village. By the time of this picture it would pass two large mansions built by the Backhouse banking family and designed by the prolific Victorian architect Alfred Waterhouse. The trees in the background are probably in Alfred Backhouse's Pilmoor park, later renamed Rockcliffe. He died in 1888.

STATION TERRACE, CROFT SPA.   No 1111.

27   On entering Hurworth at the Blind Lane corner was a pump. This was replaced in 1911 by the drinking fountain 'erected by Alice and Maude Scurfield to commemorate the accession of H.M. George V.'. These ladies were the daughter and daughter-in-law of Colonel George Scurfield of Hurworth House, now a preparatory school. Behind the pump, the handsome National School of hammer-dressed sandstone built in 1831 on a new site was enlarged in 1877 and again in 1895. It replaced a school of 1770 supported by the Lord Crewe Trust. After closure about 1960 it became the church hall until converted into four dwellings. Opposite at Glen Lee lived genial William Chisholm, village doctor for thirty-seven years, who died in 1906. He considered the mild climate of Hurworth superior to that of Bournemouth.

28 The Tithe Barn for Hurworth parish, which included Neasham, was photographed during demolition in 1879. It was sited between the oldest parsonage dated 1450 at Cross Bank and the Old Rectory of classical style built in stone and facing Chapel Green by the Reverend Robert Hopper Williamson in the early 19th century. The oak timber of the Tithe Barn's 13th century cruck frames was used for making new choir stalls after the chancel of All Saints parish church was rebuilt during a church restoration of 1871.

29 The Green, here being used for informal football, used to extend down to the river. Village greens were traditionally both common grazing grounds and places for recreation. Hurworth Green was said to be last grazed at the beginning of this century by a goat which got into the Reading Room of the old Parsonage, apparently hungry for news, and ate the Northern Echo. Old customs included Christmas sword dancers, mummers and an August Bank Holiday Bean Feast, the beans being eaten on Sunday evening before Monday's fair. In 1897, Queen Victoria's Diamond Jubilee was celebrated with tea, races, mugs for the children, a bonfire and fireworks. Trees were planted on the Green for her Golden and Diamond Jubilees and for the Coronation of King Edward VII. Daffodils are now a feature.

Hurworth. The Green

30 Hurworth doctors served the local spas, and analysed the waters. Dr. William Chisholm, pictured around 1900 driving along the green in his trap, was a familiar figure. According to Dr. Fothergill, he was a physician of the old school and did a roaring trade with Croft Spa on the one hand and Dinsdale Spa on the other, so much so that 'he was for many years never seen except in the act of mounting a horse or alighting from one, so rapid was his flight between one patient's residence and that of another'. He also wrote about the poor health of Hurworth's linen weavers and the accidents to those who became railway navvies, unused as they were to heavy manual labour and outdoor work. Government House, the tall house behind, was a 19th century stamp and post agency.

Apricot trees used to grow over the fronts of many of the houses.

31   The green peters out towards the east end. The Bay Horse coaching inn on the left possibly dates from the 15th century. Its sundial marked 1739 over the archway is thought to be a product of Hurworth's eminent mathematician William Emerson (1701-1782). At the corner of Coach Lane the one-storey building on Church View near the old car was a smithy, and is now a motor showroom. The east end of the village, named Church Row on both sides of the street, was where mainly agricultural labourers, craftsmen and weavers used to live. A lych gate for the churchyard was built in 1898 to the memory of Colonel Scurfield of Hurworth House.

HURWORTH-ON-TEES   No 508.

32   Church Row had several shops. The large signboard on the left proclaims Clarkson's Tea, Coffee, Grocery, Provisions & Family Supply Stores. J.P. Clarkson also had a shop in Darlington in the 1890s. This one had been built in 1878 as a Village Hall with a reading room and billiard room by Miss Scurfield who applied for permission as a Cocoa Room, Coffee Palace or Coffee Tavern. Latterly the WI met upstairs, it housed a bakery and now a dentist. The strange porch has gone, but there are traces of former Victorian Gothic arches. The row of four with box-like shop windows had a saddler's, a paper shop and Hay's grocery which began as a bakery opposite. The whole long upper floor of the four was a ballroom! The flat shop window was Bert Bell's, the butcher, and at the end was blacksmith Dick Sanderson's. The distant houses edging the road were demolished.

HURWORTH-ON-TEES.

Nº 1122.

33   Seen here from the Yorkshire bank of the Tees, Hurworth stands high. Below the church and its flood wall appear outcrops of red sandstone in the river bank. The former All Saints church of 12th century date had a chancel, nave, aisles, a porch and a low west tower. In 1831-32 the church was almost entirely rebuilt with transepts, galleries and 830 seats to cope with a greatly increased population. In 1871 came another substantial rebuilding, by Darlington architect J.P. Pritchett, with a much enlarged chancel and the removal of galleries. Little of antiquity remains apart from the medieval piers and the 15th century tower. The distant buildings are down the steep gardens and yards behind Church Row. The private iron cart-bridge was built in 1879 to carry sewage from Hurworth to land then owned by Lord Rokeby, the cost being shared.

34 The east end of Hurworth used to house linen weavers, labourers, gardeners, blacksmiths, cartwrights, joiners, masons, boot and shoe makers and shopkeepers. Many of the workshops in this picture of circa 1905 have now gone. From around 120 workers in 1830, linen weaving ended with elderly men in the 1870s. The last two looms were in a 'subterranean room'. Working in cellars gouged from the rock or damp sheds, many weavers had tuberculosis. Younger men opted for railway work. The mathematician Emerson designed his wife's spinning wheel and wore local linen. The weaver Dryden rose to be a captain in the Life Guards. The roof with ventilator triangles covered the Temperance Hall of 1864 which held 250 for lectures and meetings. A low building towards the left was the band practice room. Mrs. Miller remembers the band's 'Christians Awake' on Christmas mornings.

35 Before Low Hail Bridge (shown in picture number 33) was built, the Tees could be crossed at a nearby ford where rocks outcropped in the river bed. The ford was reached by a narrow lane captured here in a painting by W.H. Cooper. The lane led off Church Row between cottages opposite The Otter and Fish. A paved lane can still be distinguished, now walled off and usually overgrown with brambles. The cottages to the right between the lane and the bridge, squeezed between the road and the river and threatened by river erosion, were demolished.

36 Newbus Grange, now the Newbus Arms Hotel, was built in 1610, but received a Gothic treatment, castellations, window tracery and a cast iron verandah in the Regency period. The large bay was added after a fire in 1935. There were three cottages, a lodge, two flats in the house and three hundred acres of land which was farmed. A succession of families lived there during the 19th century. In the 1880s, Alexander Park was farming 85 acres with three labourers, six domestic servants and a coachman. The Riley-Lord family lived there after the First World War, of whom Scylla is the girl in the foreground. At one stage the house was covered in creepers.

37   Nurse Ovens is looking after the three Riley-Lord daughters, the eldest being Scylla. She recalls that in the 1920s and 1930s there were three gardeners, three stables workers and eight indoor staff comprising the butler, lady's maid, parlourmaid, cook, three housemaids and a nursery maid.

38   The road between Hurworth and Neasham was reputedly haunted by Hob Headless, who was unable to cross the Kent Beck. Entry into Neasham is over Kent Bridge. The road and bridge were widened in 1970/71, and these stone parapets replaced by fawn brick ones. On the left are cottages built for the market gardens about 1850. Opposite was the High Wath or ford where each Bishop of Durham was greeted by the falchion ceremony until 1790, when the ford became unsafe through the removal of gravel from the bed of the Tees. After the village flood embankment was built in 1968, and heightened later, a paved riverine walk to Sockburn Lane was laid out along the bank top beside the Kent and the Tees.

39   The Kent, Cree and Bowbridge Becks drain the low ground where the skeleton of an elk drowned in a peaty pool just after the Ice Age was found in 1939. The Miller family farms this land behind the village. Harry Miller came to Skip Bridge Farm around 1928 and moved to Neasham Springs circa 1939. Both farms were formerly part of the Lloyd Pease's Hurworth Moor estate. Harry poses here at Skipbridge with his son Norman, wife Ellen and daughter Jessie. To the left is a visiting old school friend, Mrs. Hurst, with her children Marjorie and Henry. Skip Bridge farmhouse has an old left side with a for-mer gable entrance and Flemish brickwork. The right side extension has English bond with five stretcher rows for each header row (see picture 52). Upstairs are traditional Yorkshire sliding sash windows. Harry removed the ivy. Norman married in 1950 and moved in 1964 to Neasham Springs (built 1895) when Harry retired.

40 The Fox and Hounds was built in 1835. Its signboard here depicts the Hurworth Hunt. The earlier ground floor windows have been enlarged and straight steps replaced by two flights. On the right is a National Cyclists' Union sign. The buildings have now been much extended. The gardens to the right became first a car park and now have a conservatory dining room and outdoor sitting area. The path to the left is Slipway Lane which led past a boat house and rope loft to a ferry over the Tees. This was operating in the 17th century when it was complained that the boat maintained by the lord of the manor was missing. The ferry ceased in 1906.

41   Low-lying, on the outer swing of an acute meander, Neasham village was vulnerable to floods. In moderate inundations, pedestrians used the raised pavement which continued as a railed walk and steps where the road level was lowered in the 1880s. Beside it is the market gardener's house, stable and loft rebuilt on the old cobbled cellars and walls after the disastrous flood of 1771. Just beyond the children and the market garden semis, the Jubilee Pump was set into the orchard wall for Queen Victoria's Golden Jubilee. It was removed in 1932 to make way for Allison's private bus garage. Elmtree Cottage, now without the elm, was Warwick's grocery and post office. The single storey cottage later became a post office and store, now closed and two storeyed. The Low Wath ford to the left, made after the High Wath became untenable, is still used.

THE TEES IN FLOOD AT NEASHAM, JUNE 10th, 1914.

42 These terraced houses were grouped round two communal yards. The gap on the left, now called Ford View, led to the smithy behind. There was a post office in the first part, just off the picture to the left. The next part included the Hare and Hounds with a stable and brewhouse behind. This pub closed in 1955. The end premises were a shop, post office and cobbler's workshop. Village post offices tended to move to whoever would take them on! Beyond is ivy-covered Ivy House, built in the 1880s with four steps to raise it above floods. It had a carriage entrance, stables, gardens, a cottage and out-houses at the rear. It also incorporated older farm buildings at right angles to the road. The rough state of the village green is apparent in this picture dated 1909.

43　The end terrace shop window has gone, and Ivy House next door has no ivy! Ivy House was relieved of its ivy in 1935 and divided into two in 1938. The two Wellingtonias in its rear garden were for long a landmark. First one went, then in the 1990s, the other. To the right are the two-storey preacher's house adjoining a one storey cottage chapel which was active until the late 1980s. The Methodist New Connexion was established in Neasham in 1796. In their place are now four new houses with the drawing rooms upstairs to give a view over the flood protection bank. Next on the right is the village school teacher's house. Seats were placed on the green for the Coronations of George V in 1911 and George VI in 1937, and bulbs planted for Queen Elizabeth's Coronation in 1953 and Silver Jubilee in 1977. In 1960 the green was levelled up and Neasham won the Tidy Village competition.

44   This winter picture is probably of a similar date to that of picture number 42. The green is railed and grazed, but the river is spilling over the lower part. Beyond, beside the river, trees indicate one of the four orchards and market gardens which gave work in Neasham. On the hill behind is Neasham Hill House, built about 1757, which, like Neasham Hall and Abbey House, also provided local work. The green remained rough until after the Second World War, when the Durham County Plan of 1952 designated Neasham a Category D Village. It was to have no further investment and to be allowed to die.

Once mains sewerage had been installed in 1958-1964, however, and a flood protection embankment built in 1968, Neasham developed as a desirable residential village.

45   This flood picture looks east across the green towards the most acute part of the Tees bend. The place-name Neasham comes from Anglo-Saxon 'naes' meaning a nose or headland. It was thought that this flood of 1968 would be the last great flood, after which the embankment was built. Disaster struck again, however, early in 1995 when the river backed up the becks at either end of the village and flooded it from behind, inundating the houses and bungalows along Teesway to a depth of several feet. The Tees, indeed, had its way once again. The notorious flood of 1771 did enormous damage along the whole length of Teesdale. Neasham itself, however, appears to have suffered worse in 1753, when it was reported that all except one house was destroyed and cattle and stacks of hay and corn were swept away. But most references to rebuilding the village seem to relate to 1771.

46   Neasham Feast was held on the green on August Bank Holiday weekend, the first weekend in August, until the mid-1920s. It was fun time, with competitions, coconut shies, as seen in the foreground, and amusement stalls. The Crow family fairground toured the region from their base in Middlesbrough. Founded before the First World War by Sam Crow, who began by playing in Milburn's Brass Band, the firm has now passed down three generations of Crows. After moving to Northallerton for machine threshing during the Second World War, the Crows overwinter their apparatus on the Applegarth.

The stall in the background appears to read 'A. Crow's latest repeating rifle', and the roundabout is a Crow. Former schoolteacher Anne Lee remembers Crow's roundabouts and Granny Noble's brittle yellow Cinder Toffee!

47   The village school began as a National (C of E) School in 1870 with a donation of land and money by Mr. Chapman Ward of Neasham Hill House. There were two schoolrooms for 107 children and a single-storey teachers' house. Two sisters taught there in the 1880s. In 1889 the house was raised to two storeys, the ground floor connecting to the school as an overflow schoolroom. In 1927 it became a County Council all-age school, but from 1938 primary only when the seniors went to Hurworth. It closed in 1961 and became a private house the following year, not greatly altered on the outside. PT (physical training) lessons were held on the village green!

48   Facing the wall of the large market garden on the right was a row of twelve cottages, rebuilt after the 1771 flood with river cobbles and brick. Some probably housed linen weavers, of whom six remained in Neasham in the mid 19th century. The signboard indicates The Golden Cock, a pub which thrived until closure in 1958. Also in the row was Soakell's grocery shop which closed about 1970. Three adjacent cottages remained until the 1980s, including the one with the grocery's box-like shop window. These were revamped into two houses. At the far end of the row was the Home Farm for Neasham Hill House. About 1900, houses at the near end of the row, at the Sockburn cross roads, were demolished to make way for model houses, one of which is seen on the left of the picture.

NEASHAM, NEAR DARLINGTON.

Nº 1123.

49   Here on the corner are some of the model houses built in 1901-02 by Sir Thomas Wrightson of Neasham Hall after seeing a model estate in the London area. To the left, facing the Sockburn Lane, two of the houses act as wings to a village Reading Room designed with two porched doors so that if not successful it could be converted into houses. The Room was for men. For special functions, ladies could use the adjoining house's sitting room as a cloak room! Soldiers were billetted in the Room during the First World War, after which the WI, founded in 1916, moved in and still meets there. A War Memorial tree and Roll of Honour were placed in the corner garden. The Roll is now indoors. In 1955 Sir John Wrightson donated the premises to the village. The hunt is probably the long established Hurworth Hunt, which moved away to the Cleveland area.

50   Rounding the corner below Neasham Hill, the sack-laden horse and cart is passing the criss-cross fencing and cobbled pavement of the model houses. The one-storey house on the left, now stripped of its limewash and with an added porch, is named The Weaver's Cottage. A pump in the usual upright casing can be seen in the rear of the Pump House shelter. Entwined initials and a Latin inscription record that it was the gift of Ronald and Samuel Ward in 1879. The pump itself has gone, but a villager recalled that the water spout was like the Sockburn Worm. Neasham Hill House the home of the Wards was built around 1757, and a wing added in 1877. There was a vinery, and the gardens spread downhill to the Sockburn Lane and included the gardener's Dutch-gabled cottage. Mr. Cresswell Ward sold off most of the Wards' cottages after the First World War.

51 William Wrightson bought 400 acres along the Sockburn Lane in 1803. He built the first Neasham Hall as a family home, laid out the estate, planted the woodland and river banks and rebuilt much of the village, adding a garden to every cottage. In 1834 his son Thomas sold the estate to Colonel James Cookson who rebuilt the Hall to the design of John Dobson. The grandson, Sir Thomas Wrightson, of the Head Wrightson bridge building firm, Teesside, repurchased the estate in 1891. He built the model cottages and Reading Room at Neasham, the gate lodge for the Hall, a dower house at Eryholme and a private bridge linking it to the Hall. He died in 1921, outliving his brother The Reverend Garmonsway Wrightson, vicar of Hurworth, who died in 1900.

The Hall was demolished in 1970 and replaced by a smaller one.

52   The heavy clays around Neasham were suitable for making bricks and drainage tiles. Clay dug from a claypit was packed into wooden moulds, each brick being cut by wire and baked in brick ovens as seen in this picture of Neasham brickworkers in 1924. Some houses in these villages by the Tees have very thin bricks, as in the rebuilt Emerson house in Hurworth. Impurities baked off leaving an attractive pitted and varicoloured surface and a slightly irregular shape. Machine cutting brought greater regularity. Usually in this area, bricks were laid in modified English bond, rows of headers separated by three or five rows of stretchers. Many houses, however, were of the Flemish bond popular around 1800, with every row in alternate headers and stretchers. Header bond, using entirely headers for expensive display as at Hurworth Old Hall, is unusual hereabouts.

53   Neasham brickworks provided an extra type of work available for local men. Closure typically resulted in a flooded claypit and overgrown banks. Indecision about what to do with the site meant that wildlife had a chance to colonise and become established. Eventually the site has become a nature reserve and educational resource.

54 Life in a First World War army camp at Neasham was illustrated in postcards, with doggerel verse. This one, 'From One of the Boys in Khaki' illustrates boxing, trenching, parade, the hungry queue and a field kitchen. 'In Khaki dressed we'll hunt the Hun, And show him the Colour that does not run.' Another card, 'Just a Kindly Thought from Our Camp at Neasham', shows bayonet drill, a football match, the tents and physical drill. 'My Greetings true I send to you, Their Sincerity needs no explanation, We show you here just what we do, To keep ourselves in training.'

55   Sockburn lies isolated at the end of the longest and most complicated of the Tees meanders. The 13th century church on Saxon foundations was all but demolished in 1838 when Girsby church across the river was opened. Part was rebuilt in 1900 to house local sculptured stones, including the effigy of a knight, perhaps Sir John Conyers of Sockburn Worm fame. In the field are mounds, the remnants of the village and hall of the Conyers, and not far away a grey stone beneath which the Worm was by legend buried. The site was important in Saxon times, possibly having a minster for a large estate. Higbald was consecrated Bishop of Lindisfarne here in 780 A.D. Sockburn Hall was rebuilt in 1834 by the Blacketts of Matfen. Theophania Blackett built an iron girder bridle bridge over the Tees to replace a way past the hall.

56 The H.A.W. Cocks Memorial Homes, 1905, were built with a bequest by Mr. Cocks of Low Middleton Hall. Since this early picture, the cupola has been replaced by a pyramid roof, the chimney pots and iron railings have gone and the clock is now electric, but a cast iron pump remains. The Cocks of Plymouth inherited the Killinghall's ancient manor of Middleton St. George. Henry Andrew William Cocks, the last lord, presided for most of the 19th century. In 1860 he founded blast furnaces and an ironworks alongside the Stockton and Darlington Railway near Fighting Cocks station. These were followed by a wire works in 1882, a brick works and a railway wagon repair works, whereupon a new village of Middleton St. George emerged to house and serve the workers some distance from the old church and lost medieval village. Henry Cocks subscribed to a new church and schools. After his death in 1894, his lands were broken up and sold.

DINSDALE ALMS HOUSES.   No 1557.

57   The focus of The Square was the cast iron drinking trough around the central gas lamp. The Middleton and Dinsdale Gas Company was founded in 1871, and by the 1990s Middleton had thirty-two public lamps. The Central Buildings beyond led round to Station Road, Neasham Road and Church Lane. On the right, the corner shop with a Pullars of Perth cleaners' sign, is now Hills' post office and newsagents, and there was a cobbler's shop. The wooden shed was a children's clothes shop and later became Holloways fruit shop. Now rebuilt, it houses a betting office, with the Havelock Arms still next door. On the left, the Killinghall Arms pub has an elaborate gas lamp over the door.

MIDDLETON ST. GEORGE

58 Central Buildings is named on a plaque above the shop door near which a child is bending over a two-handled box cart. The right hand shop doorway reads Post Office and the windows show an array of bottles and packets. 'John Bowes sold everything, and ran a Brooke Bonds Tea van.' Next door is a long striped barber's pole. Round the corner on Station Road the Co-op came later, and closed. The road continues and rises on a bridge over the railway. The shop on the left advertises Fry's Chocolate in enamelled lettering, and is remembered as Dunns' shop. Central Buildings were demolished, and two police houses with their office were built in their place. The houses are now private. The older houses on the left are still there.

CENTRAL BUILDINGS, DINSDALE.   Nº 1559.

59 At the Killinghall Arms, F.A. Rhodes was licensed to retail British and foreign spirits, ale, porter and tobacco. On the left, the window above the stained glass Smoke Room panel advertises Burton's Pale Ale and Charrington's, whilst on the right, BOS Scotch Whiskey. Dark Venetian blinds and lace curtains upstairs reflect the period. The shop on the left was, at this time, Middleton St. George Post Office. The fascia board names M. Brough grocer and provision dealer, with Fry's Chocolate on each of the four window panels. In the window are rows of boiled sweets in glass jars. It is now a Chinese Takeaway.

The fascia board on the right names Dees, grocer and provision dealer. The window has (brown?) teapots in a row, an enamelled jug and basin, packets and small jars. Was ZE for Zebo or Zebra? Each window panel has an oiled cloth blind. This shop later became Ferguson's fish and chips, and is now vacant.

MIDDLETON - ST - GEORGE.

Nº 1558 .

60   Dinsdale station on Station Road at Middleton St. George was built when the line of the original Stockton and Darlington Railway of 1825 was re-routed in 1887 via Darlington Bank Top Station and Geneva Junction. Fighting Cocks Station on the original route was then closed. The nearby iron works closed between the wars and were demolished in 1947. Fighting Cocks was designated a Category D area from 1951 until re-prieved in 1970. The Dinsdale Station booking office, clock and toilets were on the railway bridge on Station Road and the waiting rooms were down on the platforms. Note the normal style of the gas lamps. The station was named Dinsdale, being just inside the Dinsdale boundary.

61   Dinsdale station is here seen from the bridge with the slope of the approach ramp on the right. The more ornate gas lamps are an attractive feature. Dinsdale station staff took a great pride in their gardens beside both platforms, and won many prizes. A post office on Station Road used to display photographs of the prizes. The picture also shows a greenhouse. There was a drinking fountain on the wall of the left hand waiting room. A clerestory NER train is approaching from the east from the Stockton direction. In the background are the terraced houses for Dinsdale iron-works families.

Dinsdale Railway Station. (First Prize for Floral Decoration)   No. 1555.

62   Colonel (later Sir) Robert Ropner and his wife gave this convalescent home and grounds in 1897 to commemorate Queen Victoria's Diamond Jubilee, and for its continued use by the workmen of Stockton and Thornaby. Seen here in its early days, it was formally opened in 1898 by the Lord Bishop of Durham. Trees and foliage now obscure this view. The men used to drink Dinsdale Spa water! Ropner, a young stowaway of German extraction, became a shipbuilder in Hartlepool. In 1888 he took over an iron and steel shipbuilding yard at North Shore, Stockton, which in the 1890s employed 1,500. He specialised in cargo-carrying tramp steamers. In later life Ropner devoted himself to shipping interests and public affairs. He was a Mayor and the first Freeman of Stockton and an M.P. He gave land to the borough for Ropner Park, and his home, Preston Park, became a museum and art gallery.

THE ROPNER CONVALESCENT HOME

63 With the development of Middleton One Row for Dinsdale Spa, Middleton St. George for industry and Dinsdale for the desirable residences of Teesside businessmen, the ancient parish church of St. George became too remote. St. Laurence's church in stone in the early English style with 300 sittings was built on the Castle Hill estate in 1871 for about £2,000 to the design of the Darlington architect J.P. Pritchett. This picture was taken somewhat later, but before the First World War memorial was inserted into the churchyard wall on the right. Most of the iron railings on the wall top have been re-moved, but the original gates are still in use, with a later iron overthrow arch still in place for a lantern. Trees now obscure this view of the church, and a hawthorn hedge replaced the fence.

ST. LAURENCE CHURCH, MIDDLETON-ST GEORGE

64   Middleton One Row, formerly named Over Middleton, is a survivor, whereas the medieval villages of Middleton St. George, West Hartburn, Dinsdale and Sockburn disappeared. Even so, it was reduced to a row of empty crofts and 'a few mud-walled cottages' until, in the 1820s, the village and inn were rebuilt and many houses added to serve the prospering Dinsdale Spa. By the 1840s there were twenty one-storey lodging houses. From the 1880s private commuter villas came to Middleton Lane and Church Lane. This picture taken from the east end shows 19th century housing on The Front. Its gentle curve faces the twelve acre green which sweeps steeply down to the Tees. The red brick Methodist chapel and four adjacent houses were built in 1872. The chapel closed in 1985 and became a house. The young sycamores and horse chestnuts are now mature and the footpath is part of the Teesdale Way.

65 The westerly end of The Front is pictured here with the Devonport Hotel on the right before a wide pediment was added to the left of the portico. Beyond is a protruding shop window. The gap with trees was the garden of the rectory. The next plot, now occupied by a new bungalow, is empty. The large farmhouse has a row of one-storey cottages beyond. These have been demolished for a new farmhouse, except for one used as a garage. Four gas lamps can be detected; two are by the Devonport. The bare young trees may just have been planted, for trees at the rectory and around St. Laurence's church are in full leaf. Elderly residents remember competitions for rolling hard boiled, coloured and decorated pace or paste eggs down the green. This custom celebrated Easter, the Paschal season. (Beamish Museum.)

66   The Devonport, rebuilt in the 1820s, was the focal point for spa visitors. Its billiard table is still advertised in this picture, on a board between the two bay windows. Balls were held. 'Trowsing' could be undertaken from the local tailor's 'trow' or primitive catamaran, two boats linked by boards from which salmon lurking under the river bank could be speared. There was a bazaar at which raffles were held of cheap Birmingham goods at four times their original price. Visitors came from Northumberland, Durham and Yorkshire. The Hurworth Hunt was begun as a private pack of harriers by the Wilkinson brothers, wealthy yeomen of Neasham Abbey, but it soon changed from hares to foxes. Between the wars, it moved into Yorkshire and the South Durham Hunt came instead. Local ladies recall as children following the hunt via Fighting Cocks and along Sadberge Road to woods since felled.

67   Viewed from the west end, the one-storey buildings next to the old farmhouse are clearer. They had been cottages and a smithy, and were demolished and a new farmhouse built on the site. Beyond the old farmhouse the gables of the rectory facing the river can be seen, set back in a garden. It once had a serious fire, exposing the roof timbers. At this end of The Front there used to be a Queens Head pub and a small school. Under the nearest of the young trees sits a lady. Various paths thread the green and lead towards the spa, and have now been restored.

68 The church of St. George gave its name to the nearby medieval village of Middleton. Of this, only a few grassy mounds remain beside a small stream near the Tees, whilst Low Middleton Hall replaced the old manor house of the Killinghalls. Alone on the fringe of Teesside International Airport, the small red sandstone church patched with brick has only a nave and chancel. The main part is thought to be 13th century although Saxon origins are claimed. About 1822, when Dinsdale spa was attracting visitors, the north wall of the nave was moved out several feet for more pews, the chancel rebuilt and the whole re-roofed in Westmorland slate. Neglected after St. Laurence's church was built, its patron and lay rector H.A.W. Cocks added in 1884 an embattled and pinnacled west tower, and the whole was restored and reseated in 1889. The tower, however, began to lean away. Declared unsafe, it was removed around 1960.

MIDDLETON ST. GEORGE CHURCH.   No. 505.

69   Dinsdale spa was discovered by Major General Lambton's workmen in 1789 when, boring for coal, a sulphurous spring 'burst forth'. By 1797 a cold bath had been built, soon followed by a warm bath and dressing rooms, all rebuilt with improvements in 1824, using stone remnants from derelict Pounteys Bridge close by. Sulphur deposits had to be scraped away, silverware tarnished and sticks could be turned into matches. The water tasted bitter and 'disgustingly nauseous', but some drank four to six tumblers full before breakfast for a shilling per week. Cures were claimed for ailments as treated at Croft Spa (picture 15). In 1829, Lord Durham built on high the 70 bedroomed Dinsdale Hotel designed by Ignatius Bonomi, and laid out walks through the riverside woods. Remote and unsuccessful, the hotel became a retreat for mental invalids, a residential special school and now a nursing home.

70 Despite beautiful views over the Vale of Cleveland and the Garden of Yorkshire, the fascinating salmon leap at fish-locks and the other 'strong allurements to the invalid', the decline of the spa continued. To boost its fortunes, the Dinsdale Improvement Company was formed in 1863, and in 1880 the bath house was rebuilt as a small hotel and baths. Decline, however, became rapid. Croft spa beside the main line station was more widely accessible, and by this time Middleton St. George and One Row had evolved in other directions. The Spa Hotel became the Club House for Dinsdale Spa Golf Club, and as that it is best remembered. After the Second World War, a newly-built club house beside the course was officially opened in 1966 by W.J. Milburn, President of the English Golf Union. The old Spa Hotel beside the Tees was later converted into five residential units.

71   The Dinsdale Spa Golf Club was set out on high ground above the riverside woods and beside the Neasham road, just beyond Lord Durham's hotel. It was a steep haul from the bath house and club house for both invalids and golfers. This picture records the Club's winners of the 1922 Newcastle Cup Competition intercounty foursomes, A.H. Grieveson and D.A. Haggie. Tweed jackets, plus fours, thick woollen socks and flat caps were the fashion, caught here like the panama hat and trilbys amongst the spectators. Well-known golfers came to give exhibition matches, including international player Bobby Locke.

72   On Captain's Day, 1935, this informal group was pictured by the river in front of the old spa Club House, still partly creeper covered. Among the back row, from the left, are: J.J. Peck (secretary), E. Pybus (greenkeeper), W. Gordon, A. Webster and W. Andrews, centre row, seated: J. Hedley, E. Mann, W. Dunne, S.N. McQuistan, G. Pugh and H. Humphries, and on the ground: E. Williamson and K. Hounam. Jackets and plus fours are still in vogue at this date.

73   This picture of a manual reaper cutting corn in the Dinsdale area was probably taken on the high ground beyond the present golf course and towards the lane from Neasham to Low Dinsdale. The woods on the left would be those hanging on the steep bank of the Tees meander between Dinsdale Bridge and the spa. There are eight or nine people and a boy and two horses, whereas farming in the fields nowadays is a lonely activity. The photographer was the Reverend James Whitehead Pattison, a curate living at Middleton One Row in the 1890s. He took a great interest in country life and recorded it, as here, in photographs. (Beamish Museum.)

74 Another of the Reverend J.W. Pattison's pictures captures farmworkers cutting oats around 1900, again with a manual reaper. One man is gathering cut oats to tie into a sheaf whilst four await the passing of the horse-drawn reaper before stooking the next row. Ongoing developments brought the reaper and binder, tractors and combine harvesters. By the 1960s farm horses, farm labourers and stooked fields were getting rare and soon disappeared. This view is from Over Dinsdale, probably from Over Dinsdale Grange farmland, looking across the Tees bank woods to the hotel-become-mental retreat perched aloft. Below, and recognisable from its position, its chimney stacks and its row of square windows, is the Spa Hotel and bath house down beside the Tees. (Beamish Museum.)

75   The parish church, rectory, school, manor house and mounds are all that remain of the old village of Low Dinsdale. The ancient manor of the Surtees family, whose name meant 'on Tees', passed into various hands but was bought by Henry George Surtees after the death of Lord Durham. Surtees gave land for the school built in 1851 for thirty children. It is now a house. In this somewhat posed picture taken by the Reverend J.W. Pattison, children are walking past the church and rectory to the school on the left. Mr. Pattison was a curate at Seaton Carew about 1890, and at Dinsdale for a year in 1891, and possibly also at Middleton. He became the vicar of St. John's Chapel in Weardale from 1906 until his death in 1936. (Beamish Museum.)

76   This view would be impossible now, the church being enshrouded with trees. The porch is no longer draped with creepers. Although there was a church here in the 7th century, the present church of St. John the Baptist was built in 1195. The large south aisle was added as St. Mary's chapel in 1200, and later renamed the Surtees chapel when Sir Alexander Surtees undertook repairs in the 14th century. The whole was restored in 1876 and the tower rebuilt. The clock was donated in 1901 by Mrs. Dixon-Johnson of Croft, and the chancel enlarged in 1908. Local red sandstone is varied by dressed stone from Osmotherley. The complete grave cover of Gocolinus Surteys who died in 1366, is mounted in the porch.

No 507.   DINSDALE CHURCH